Contents

The Jungle Book

Rudyard Kipling
Adapted by Pippa Goodhart

Illustrated by Mike Spoor

OXFORD
UNIVERSITY PRESS

CHAPTER I

—◆—

Mowgli and the wolves

Shere Khan* prowled stripy paws through hot, steamy jungle grass. Then he stopped still and sniffed. He smiled. Shere Khan, the tiger, had smelled people. He licked his lips. He looked towards a village of huts with a thorn fence nearly all the way around it. The gate in that fence was open.

Shere Khan slunk down low and crept across the field. Keeping in the shadows, he slipped through the gate and into the village. Then he wandered between the huts, wanting to be seen.

'Tiger!' screamed a woman. 'Run!'

Shere Khan was like a cat with a mouse. He liked to catch food that was running. It was good sport. Shere Khan growled, opening his mouth wide and lifting his head so that the growl rolled around the village.

'Run for your lives!' shouted an old man. 'Quick!'

Everybody ran into the village huts and slammed doors shut. But they had left somebody outside. Out by the fire, a baby boy sat in the dust, and he saw something he hadn't seen before. He pointed at the big, loud tiger and he laughed!

The baby got up onto his stumpy legs and began to toddle towards the tiger, wanting to touch its stripy fur.

Shere Khan prepared to pounce. Then he leaped! But the baby had stumbled down behind the fire, so, when Shere Khan leaped after him, he landed in the flames! Snarling with fury, Shere Khan jumped from the fire, licking his burnt paws. And the baby boy stumbled out of the village and into the jungle.

Father Wolf was out hunting when he saw a small, naked man-cub, all on his own. Father Wolf stopped still in surprise. He watched the baby boy toddle to his wolf cave home, and tumble down right onto the warm furry huddle of Mother Wolf and her cubs.

Snuggled in the warm fur, the baby found a teat, and he suckled and drank milk from Mother Wolf. In Mother Wolf's mind, that made the boy her own child. 'What a funny little cub!' she thought.

But suddenly the wolf cave went dark as the great head of Shere Khan pushed through the opening, snarling hot, angry tiger breath. 'Where is the boy?' demanded angry Shere Khan. He lunged forward, but his shoulders couldn't fit through the hole.

Mother Wolf grabbed her children and the man-cub by the scruffs of their necks and she dropped them at the back of the cave, out of reach of those terrible tiger teeth.

'Get out and leave my children be, old tiger!' said Mother Wolf.

'But one of them is not your child!' said Shere Khan. 'That is the one that I want.'

'I won't let you kill this boy!' said Mother Wolf. 'He will grow up, and he will kill you, Shere Khan!'

The tiger roared a terrible roar that filled the cave, but he could not get in. So, away went Shere Khan on his sore paws, still growling with fury.

Mother and Father Wolf looked at the boy who had landed in their family. 'He looks like a little frog! We will call him Mowgli,'* they decided.

'Will the wolf pack accept him?' asked Mother Wolf anxiously.

'We must go to Council Rock and ask them,' said Father Wolf. 'But if the wolves will not take him as a brother, they may want to kill him.'

At Council Rock, the other wolves sniffed hungrily at Mowgli and muttered, 'He would make a tasty meal!' But Mother Wolf sent them away. All this time, little Mowgli wasn't afraid. He sat on Council Rock and played with some pebbles.

Father Wolf asked Akela,* the leader of the wolves, 'Please, O wise leader, may Mowgli join our wolf pack?'

Akela frowned. 'How will he learn how to live in the jungle?'

Then big old brown bear Baloo* came forward. He was the one who taught all the young wolves about jungle life. Baloo sniffed the man-cub, and he said gently, 'I will teach him our laws.'

'Oh, let's eat the boy, Akela!' said the other wolves. 'We're hungry.'

But suddenly something black and sleek slipped into the crowd, and the wolves quietened. It was Bagheera,* the panther, still aquiver from hunting.

Bagheera glared at the wolves and told them, 'I will buy the boy from you! Feast on the carcass of this fresh-killed bull. In return,

you must let the man-cub into your pack.'

'That is a fair price,' said Akela. 'The man-cub can stay in the wolf pack and no wolf shall harm him.'

'Thank you!' said Father and Mother Wolf. Then Mother Wolf took Mowgli home to sleep in the cave.

And, deep in the jungle, Shere Khan roared his anger into the night.

CHAPTER 2

Mowgli and the monkeys

Mowgli grew and learned with his wolf cub brothers and sisters. He learned to know the plants of the jungle, the birds and beasts. He learned the languages of them all. But, above all, Mowgli learned Jungle Law.

'Always beware of the monkeys!' said Baloo. 'Never trust a monkey. They are all liars. They are cruel and dangerous and…'

'Oh, I'm bored with all this learning, Fat Old Baloo!' said Mowgli, with a yawn.

But Baloo warned, 'If you don't learn what I tell you, you will get into terrible trouble! Oh, you young ones have much to learn!'

'Boring!' said Mowgli. 'I want to play!'

'Lessons first!' said Baloo.

But one long, hot afternoon, Baloo was snoozing off a meal of honey, and Bagheera was taking a nap, when Mowgli heard shrieks and laughter in the trees. So he went to see who was having fun.

'Boo!'

A big grey monkey swung from a tree and took Mowgli by the hand. 'Come and play with us!' he said. 'Have some nuts and meet my friends!'

Mowgli looked at the monkeys. 'I'm like you. Except that I have no tail!'

'Oh, you and us lot, we're the best!' boasted the monkey. 'We aren't like those dull, old animals on four paws. We two-legged ones know how to enjoy ourselves!' The monkey snatched some nuts and threw them at a frog to make it jump.

'Ha haa!' laughed Mowgli. 'Can I try?'

Mowgli and the monkeys chattered and played. 'This is better than lessons!' said Mowgli.

'Come with us,' laughed the monkeys. 'We'll show you what real fun is! Come on!'

Suddenly Mowgli felt himself snatched by rough monkey hands. 'No! I…!' began Mowgli.

But the monkeys swung up into the trees, carrying Mowgli with them.

'Wait!' said Mowgli. 'I don't want…'

But his breath was taken away by being hauled and swung up, up, up into the branches high above the ground. Mowgli felt sick and giddy, but excited too by the rush of air and by being so high up. He wanted to struggle free from the monkeys who held him, but he daren't in case they dropped him.

Down below, Baloo and Bagheera woke up.

'Where is the boy?'

'He's gone! The monkeys have taken him.
He's in terrible danger, Baloo!'

'Oh, if only we hadn't fallen asleep!'

But Mowgli had one friend who was higher
in the sky than he was. Chil,* the kite, flew
overhead. He looked down and saw Mowgli
and the monkeys swinging through the tree
tops. And Mowgli looked up and saw Chil.

'Tell Bagheera and Baloo where I am!'
shouted Mowgli, and off Chil flew.

'What can we do?' said Baloo when Chil
had told them where Mowgli was. 'We can't
get up into the trees, and, besides, we could
never fight a hundred monkeys between the
two of us!'

'We need Kaa* to help us,' said Bagheera.

Kaa was a mighty great python snake, long
and strong enough to squeeze the life out of
almost anything. He was keen to have a go at
the kidnapping monkeys.

Chil pointed with his beak to show the way the monkeys had gone, then Kaa set off, slithering fast through the jungle while Bagheera ran alongside. Baloo tried to run too, but a fat old bear is never as fast as a snake or a panther, so he was soon left behind.

The monkeys took Mowgli to the Lost City* that had once been around the great palace of an Indian king. But now the city's ruins were mixed with jungle in a muddle of walls and trees and creepers.

'This is our home,' the monkeys told Mowgli. 'This is where you will teach us man language so that we can be kings in the palace!'

'But I don't speak man language!' said Mowgli. The grip of monkey hands on his arms got tighter. They twisted, hurting Mowgli.

'Let me go!' said Mowgli.

'Not until you remember man language!' said the monkeys. They dragged Mowgli with them, leaping through the ruins, quarrelling and laughing as the sun went down.

'I'm hungry,' said poor Mowgli.

'Oh, we've got food,' laughed the monkeys. They showed Mowgli nuts and pawpaws, then they snatched the food away and stuffed it into their own mouths.

As night darkened, Mowgli called into the jungle, 'Baloo! Bagheera!'

But there was no reply. Alone and very scared, Mowgli thought, 'Baloo was right about the monkeys'.

CHAPTER 3

'Kaa, the terrible python!'

The moon rose high and the hundreds of monkeys chattered in the trees and on the walls all around.

'I want to go to sleep,' said Mowgli. But the monkeys thought that was funny too. They pretended to yawn, then they did monkey sniggers and went on with their noise.

What Mowgli didn't know was that Kaa and Bagheera were already there, watching from the dark and deciding how to rescue him.

'There are hundredsss of monkeys against only two of ussss,' said Kaa. 'It will take me a while to get to where I can best strike them.'

'But they may hurt Mowgli at any moment!' said Bagheera. 'When that cloud goes over the moon, I will attack.'

The cloud moved, and so did Bagheera, pouncing amongst the monkeys and making them scream with rage and fear. Hundreds of monkeys leaped on the panther while others grabbed Mowgli and pushed him down through a roof into a room full of snakes. Mowgli knew how to land well, and he knew how to talk to snakes.

'Pleasssse don't hurt me,' he said.

'We won't,' promised the cobras. 'But don't you sssstep on us!'

So Mowgli stood amongst the snakes and listened to the sounds of fighting up above. Bagheera was being bitten and torn by the monkeys, and Mowgli guessed that the great hunter was fighting for his life.

'Bagheera! Go to the water!' shouted Mowgli. 'The monkeys can't follow you there!'

So Bagheera heaved off as many monkeys as he could and he crawled towards the water,

fighting all the way. But then another voice called into the jungle night. 'I'm coming, Bagheera, my old friend!' It was Baloo, arriving at last after hurrying all night to follow his friends.

Mowgli heard the splash of Bagheera plunging into the water. And he heard the howls of the monkeys as big furry Baloo waded amongst them and threw monkey after monkey aside. Then suddenly there came another sound of whacking and thumping. Now the monkeys shrieked in great fear.

'It is Kaa, the terrible python! Run!'

Kaa was whipping his great body this way and that. 'Hissss!'

'Run!'

After a time the noise got less. Mowgli clasped his hands together. Who had died? Then he heard a familiar voice.

'Where is our little Mowgli?' asked tired Baloo.

'Trapped down here!' called Mowgli.

Kaa dangled his long, strong body down

into the snake pit and Mowgli climbed up it.

'You've been hurt!' said Mowgli when he saw the blood on Bagheera and Baloo. 'And it is my fault for following the monkeys!'

'It is your fault,' agreed Baloo. 'And this snake, Kaa, came to your rescue even though he doesn't know you, Mowgli. You owe him your life.'

'Thank you, Kaa,' said Mowgli.

'Now,' said Bagheera. 'A lesson has been learned. Get up onto my back and we will all go home.'

Mowgli lay on the warm panther's back and slept all the way back to his home-cave.

CHAPTER 4

Treasure

One evening, Mowgli saw that Kaa had shed his skin, and he knew that Kaa would be feeling thin-skinned and sorry for himself. So Mowgli went to cheer him up.

Kaa relaxed his great coils to make a ring for Mowgli to sit on as if it was an armchair.

'How does my new skin look?' asked Kaa.

Mowgli stroked a hand over it. 'It is a very beautiful skin,' he told Kaa. 'But the colours will show better when they are wet. Let's go swimming. I'll carry you to the pool!'

This was a game they both knew well. Mowgli tried to lift the great length and weight

of the python, but couldn't, and Kaa knocked
him over and wrapped him tight in his coils.
Mowgli struggled until Kaa suddenly let go,
and Mowgli fell onto the grass.

'Haa! I'll get you next time!' promised
Mowgli.

They sank silently into the dark water pool
and floated. Mowgli was on his back, watching
the moon rising behind the trees.

'What could be better than this?' asked
Mowgli.

'I wonder,' said Kaa. 'There is something in the ruined city that a true man-boy would think better than this.'

'What's that?' asked Mowgli. 'Food?'

'No,' said Kaa. 'It is something guarded by the old white cobra. He said that I could bring my man-friend to see it.'

'Then let's go!' said Mowgli, climbing out of the pool and shaking himself.

The ruined city was empty, its crumbling walls lit by the moonlight.

'This way,' said Kaa, and he slipped down a hole that went underground. Mowgli dropped to his knees and followed, crawling through the darkness.

They came to a large den, lit slightly from above through cracks made by tree roots. Mowgli could see movement, and, as his eyes got used to the gloom, he saw the biggest cobra he had ever seen. The snake was completely white because it never saw sunlight. Its eyes were red as berries. It had guarded this den since the times when kings lived in the city. Mowgli bowed low to show respect for the old snake.

'Do you sssssee my treasure?' hissed the snake.

Mowgli looked around. 'No,' said Mowgli.

'Do you not ssssee?' asked the snake angrily.

Mowgli reached down and picked up a handful of metal discs that shone when held in the light.

'Can you eat these?' asked Mowgli. 'Or wear them, or shelter under them? I see no value in these.'

Mowgli was standing on a vast hoard of gold and silver coins. Amongst the coins were dishes and weapons and furniture and statues and rings and much more. All were made of gold and silver and ivory, and decorated with amber and jade and turquoise, and emeralds and pearls and rubies and diamonds and garnets.

Mowgli scowled at them, and picked up just one thing. It was a stick with a kind of claw at one end. It was decorated all over with jewels, but it was the sharp hook that took Mowgli's fancy because he thought it could make a useful tool.

'Ah, sssso you do want some of my treasure!' said the snake.

'I can see some use for this claw-stick,' said Mowgli.

'Hisss!' The white cobra nodded to something else on the floor; the skulls of two dead men. 'Those men wanted to take my treasure, but I made sure they took nothing – not even their own lives – out of here! Sssstart running, man-cub!'

Kaa whipped his body between the cobra and Mowgli. 'You invited me to come and bring the man-cub with me! You can't kill him!'

'Oh, yessss I can!'

But, quick as a snake strike, Mowgli flung the stick so that it pinned the white cobra to the floor.

'Now kill him with your knife, Mowgli!' said Kaa.

But Mowgli shook his head. 'No,' he said. 'There is no need. Look in there.' Mowgli prised open the cobra's great mouth, and they could see that the poison fangs had aged and withered. 'He cannot kill us,' said Mowgli. 'We are safe to let him go.' Mowgli pulled the hooked stick free.

'Go!' hissed the white cobra. 'Take that claw-stick with you. Death will go with it, death to all greedy mankind!'

Mowgli and Kaa hurried out of the tunnel, up into good jungle air and light. Mowgli was pleased with the way that the stick glittered its colours in the moonlight.

'Almost as pretty as flowers!' he said. 'I will take it to show Bagheera. Farewell, Kaa.'

CHAPTER 5

— ◆ —

'A cruel thing'

Bagheera was drinking at the pool. 'What have you there, little brother?' he asked.

'A strange thing of little use,' said Mowgli.

'I like the coloured stones,' said Bagheera.

'They make the claw-stick heavy,' said Mowgli. 'I prefer my little sharp stone that fits so easily in my hand.'

'I have seen a claw-stick like this one before,' said Bagheera. 'It is what men call an ankus. They use that sharp claw to control elephants. It is a cruel thing.'

'That's horrible!' said Mowgli. 'If I'd known that, I wouldn't have taken it!' And he threw the ankus away into the jungle, and then wiped his hands clean on some damp grass.

Then Mowgli clambered high into a tree and wove creepers into a hammock,* which he lay in, and slept.

Bagheera woke Mowgli next morning. 'Your claw-stick has gone,' he told Mowgli. 'See these tracks? A man has taken it.'

'Good!' said Mowgli. 'But I wonder whether the white cobra was right. I wonder if that thing does take death with it?'

So Mowgli and Bagheera followed the man's tracks to see what had happened to him. Very soon, the tracks of those two feet were joined by another pair of feet, following and hiding, and then jumping out. And then they found a man's dead body with an arrow in it, but there was no ankus beside the man's body.

'The murderer stole your ankus,' said Bagheera. 'I wonder what has happened to him?'

So again Mowgli and Bagheera followed the new track, and soon those tracks were overcome by four other pairs of feet, and there was another body, but again no ankus. Panther and boy followed the four tracks now. First they came to a single body of a man killed with a knife. Then they found three bodies together, killed by poison.

'These three men must have killed the first man, but he must have already poisoned their food,' said Mowgli. 'What a lot of killing for one cruel stick!'

The ankus was on the ground beside the three poisoned men.

'The white cobra was right,' said Mowgli. 'That claw-stick carries death with it for greedy mankind.' Mowgli picked up the ankus, holding it at a distance. 'I shall take it back to the cobra and end this killing.'

So Mowgli took the ankus back to the ruined city. He dropped it down through a crack in the earth and it fell back onto the hoard of gold and jewels. He shouted down to the white cobra, 'Guard your king's treasure better next time, old snake! Keep those murderous things safely hidden!'

Then Mowgli went back to his jungle friends, and was glad that he was not a man-boy.

CHAPTER 6

——◆◆◆——

'You will never catch me, Shere Khan'

At night Mowgli often went prowling with
Bagheera, hunting and learning about the
jungle. One night, Bagheera let Mowgli peep
through the trees at the village, and he told
Mowgli, 'You are a man-cub, Mowgli, and one
day you must go back to living as a man.'

But Mowgli wasn't interested. His family
and friends were wolves and a bear and a
panther and a snake. But he did have an
enemy in the jungle too. Shere Khan, the
tiger, had never stopped wanting to kill
Mowgli. Cunning Shere Khan sneered at the
other wolves. 'Fancy letting a little man-cub

into your pack! Are you scared of him? You had better let me kill him for you.'

Bagheera heard what Shere Khan said, and he warned Mowgli, 'Go into the village and take their Red Flower. The Red Flower is a friend to humans, but it is feared by all animals. Take some and keep it with you.'

What Bagheera called the Red Flower was what we call fire. That night, Mowgli crept down the hill. He waded over the river, and sneaked over the fields of crops, and into the village. He crept amongst the shadows until he saw a boy holding a pot with fire in it.

Mowgli snatched the pot and cradled its heat in his hands as he ran back to the jungle. Mowgli knew that the fire was a creature that needed care if it wasn't to die. He fed it twigs and he gently blew on the fire in the pot as he had seen the people in the village blow on theirs.

Bagheera told Mowgli, 'Have a good strong branch ready by you, so that you can light it with the Red Flower when the time comes.'

And the time did come very soon. At the next council meeting, Shere Khan tried to take leadership of the pack from old Akela. But Mowgli asked, 'Why should a tiger be a leader of wolves?'

Shere Khan growled at Mowgli. 'And why should a man-cub live amongst wolves?' Then Shere Khan spoke to the wolves. 'Kill him!'

But Akela was angry with Shere Khan. 'The man-cub has lived and learned with our own cubs. He is our brother in all but blood!' Akela told the other wolves. 'If you must send Mowgli away, let him go to live with his own kind in the village. I tell you, no wolf must ever harm him. We made a promise when Bagheera bought the boy's life for a bull carcass, and we will keep that promise.'

But the other wolves still skulked low with their hackles* raised. Mowgli could see that some of them still wanted to hunt and kill him, so he thrust the stick into his pot of fire.

'If you do not want me because I am a man, then I will act like a man!'

Mowgli picked up the pot of fire. He threw it to the ground where it flared, making the wolves whimper with fear and back away. Mowgli picked up his flaming branch and he waved it around the dark shadows. He told the wolves, 'Since you hate me, I will go and live with men. But I will never betray you as you have betrayed me!'

Then Mowgli thrust the burning stick towards Shere Khan. 'And you will never catch me, Shere Khan!'

The fire singed the tiger's whiskers, making him cower and howl. Shere Khan turned and

fled into the night. The wolf pack followed him, all except for Mowgli's wolf mother and father and his wolf brothers and sisters, who stayed.

Akela and Bagheera stayed with Mowgli too. Mowgli sank down onto the ground and he cried. 'I will miss you and I will miss the jungle so much!'

'But it will be a new adventure, living with people,' said Baloo.

CHAPTER 7

In the village

So Mowgli went looking for a village where
he might find a home. He jog-trotted down
the valley and across the plain. At the gate to
the first village, Mowgli met a man. Mowgli
pointed to his own mouth to show that he
was hungry, but the man ran into the village,
shouting, 'There's a strange, naked boy with
long hair at our gate, and he can't talk!'

The people of the village came running to
see, pointing and shouting and laughing at
Mowgli. 'They are just like the monkey tribe,'
thought Mowgli.

But one woman came forward to look

closely at Mowgli. She said, 'You are very like my baby boy who was taken by the tiger all those years ago. Come and live with me. I will call you Nathoo, like my other boy.'

The woman, who was called Messua, took Mowgli into a hut. There he saw a bed and a grain chest, copper cooking pots, a mirror on the wall, and all sorts of other things that were very strange to a boy who had lived in a cave. The hut felt like a trap to Mowgli, but Messua gave him bread and milk.

'I must learn to live as a man-boy,' thought Mowgli.

Mowgli tried to learn some people language.

'Milk,' said Messua.

'Meelk,' said Mowgli.

'Good boy,' said Messua.

At bedtime, Messua's husband shut the door of the hut, making it feel even more like a trap. So Mowgli jumped out of the window and went and lay down on the grass outside. Soon a wet nose nudged him.

'Grey Brother!' said Mowgli. It was his eldest wolf brother. 'How are my wolf family?'

'They are well,' said Grey Brother. 'But I came to warn you. Shere Khan is out to kill you. I will let you know if I hear what he plans.'

'Thank you, brother,' said Mowgli.

For three months, Mowgli tried to learn to live like a man-boy. He wore clothes like the other people. He learned their language. He tried to understand about money. He learned how to plough land. The other children in the village pointed and laughed at Mowgli because he was as odd to them as they were to him. And the men of the village told Mowgli off because he had no understanding of village manners.

One day, old Buldeo, the village elder,* was telling stories under a peepul tree.* He told the story of a tiger who stole a small boy. He said that the tiger was the ghost* of a wicked old man from the village.

'Ha haa!' laughed Mowgli. 'You foolish man! That tiger is a real tiger, not a ghost of a man! The tiger is called Shere Khan.'

Buldeo's face went red. He pointed at Mowgli. 'Prove it's a real tiger!' he said. 'Bring us the skin and we might believe you!'

Because Mowgli was so cheeky, they sent him out of the village, herding the big blue-black buffalo with their back-curving horns. Mowgli liked sitting on the big bull buffalo, taking the herd out to wallow in the muddy river all day.

Out by the buffalo wallow, one day Grey Brother came to Mowgli with news.

'Shere Khan plans to catch and kill you this evening, Mowgli. He is resting in the valley, waiting for sunset and for you to go home.'

'Then it is time to act,' said Mowgli. 'Will you help me, Grey Brother?'

'I will. And so will somebody else.' Grey Brother nodded towards a rock behind Mowgli, and Mowgli turned to see a big grey head he knew well.

'Akela!'

Mowgli and the two wolves divided the buffalo herd in two, one group of cows and

calves, and another of buffalo bulls.

'Take the cows and calves to the top of the valley,' Mowgli told Grey Brother. 'Akela and I will herd the bulls in at the other end.'

Mowgli's plan was to trap Shere Khan between the two herds of buffalo. The walls of the valley were so steep, no tiger could climb them.

Mowgli and Akela slowly steered the bulls in a wide circle before heading for the valley. As they entered the valley, Mowgli put his hands on either side of his mouth and shouted so that it echoed between the rock walls.

'Tiger, where are you? I have come for you!'

'Who calls?' asked the sleepy voice of Shere Khan.

'It is I! Mowgli!'

Then Akela gave a hunting call to make the buffalo charge. Hooves raced, stones and dust flew, horns clashed and great bodies rushed forward, faster and faster. Like an avalanche* of great, grey, living boulders, the buffalo filled the valley and ran, not caring that something

soft and stripy was trampled under them.

The buffalo bulls met the cows and calves and they stopped still. But behind them was Mowgli, touching the still but warm body of the tiger. Shere Khan was dead.

'I will have your skin, Shere Khan,' said Mowgli. He pulled out his knife, sliced open the tiger skin and tugged it off Shere Khan.

Back in the village, news had come of the stampeding buffalo herd. Out came Buldeo to see what was happening. He shouted at Mowgli, 'What have you done to our herd?' Then Buldeo spotted the dead tiger. 'Is that...?'

'The ghost tiger?' laughed Mowgli. 'Now you see that he was real.'

'You will give the skin to me,' said Buldeo. 'There is a reward of one hundred rupees for this tiger's skin.' He patted Mowgli awkwardly on the shoulder. 'I shall give you one rupee of that reward for killing the beast.'

'Ha! You will not!' said Mowgli, shaking the old man away. 'Grey Brother! Akela!'

And suddenly Buldeo was knocked to the ground by two great grey wolves.

'Oh!' said Buldeo. 'Oh, Mowgli! Maharaja!* Great King! Please make them let me go!'

Mowgli signalled for his friends to let Buldeo go. 'Now, go!' Mowgli told him.

And Buldeo hobbled quickly back to the village to tell the people about the wolf-boy with magic powers to kill tigers.

When Mowgli had finally taken the whole
skin from Shere Khan's body, he set off back to
the village. In the misty twilight he could see
the people of the village gathered at the gate.
'They are going to be so glad that the man-
eating tiger is dead, they are going to welcome
me home as a hero,' thought Mowgli.

But that wasn't how the village people felt at all.

'Go away, wolf-boy!' they shouted, and they threw stones. 'Shoot him, Buldeo!'

A shot came. It missed Mowgli, but it gave a strong message.

Akela told Mowgli, 'Your man pack has turned against you.'

'Just as my wolf pack did,' said Mowgli sadly. 'The wolves don't like me because I am a man-cub, and the people don't like me because I am a wolf-boy.'

While the people herded the buffaloes back to the village, Mowgli headed back to the jungle with a wolf either side of him and a tiger skin carried on his head.

But Mowgli was happy. He no longer had to answer to a strange name or struggle with a strange language or sleep indoors!

Old Mother Wolf came out of her cave to greet Mowgli home in the moonlight.

'It is as I said it would be,' she said. 'The man-cub has killed Shere Khan.'

CHAPTER 8

Mowgli is hunted

That evening, Mowgli rested his head on Mother Wolf's flank, and he told his wolf brothers and Akela and Bagheera and Baloo about life in the man-village. He showed them the knife he had used to skin Shere Khan.

'That is indeed a sharp tooth!' said Bagheera.

'Well, man-cub,' said Father Wolf. 'You have certainly learned things.'

'But people sound such terrible creatures,' said Mother Wolf. 'Although I do like the woman for giving Mowgli shelter and milk.'

Mowgli stretched and yawned. 'I would be

very happy never to see people ever again.'

'But you will,' said Akela. 'I went back to the village. I saw men gathered and with guns in their hands. I think they plan to track you down, Little Brother. I did my best to cover the tracks we left as we came here, but that may not stop them.'

'But they sent me away!' said Mowgli. 'Why would they want to find me?'

Akela shook his grey old head. 'That I don't know,' he said. 'You are a boy, Mowgli. You should understand men better than I can.'

Mowgli glared. 'I am not a boy, I am a cub!'

Bagheera's tail twitched with irritation. 'Forget all that! Let's go hunting!'

Bagheera rose to his feet. He lifted his head and he sniffed the air. Grey Brother and the other wolves did the same.

'What is it?' asked Mowgli.

'I smell man!' said Akela.

Mowgli parted some branches and looked down into the valley. 'It is old Buldeo with his gun! He has followed us!'

Grey Brother and the other three young wolves went down on their bellies and began to hurry down the valley. 'We will kill him for you, Mowgli!'

'Stop!' said Mowgli. Mowgli glared hard into his wolf brothers' eyes until they bent their heads and cowered. 'Who is the leader of our little pack?' asked Mowgli.

'You are, brother,' said Grey Brother, and he bent and licked Mowgli's foot.

'Then follow me,' said Mowgli.

Mowgli set off down the valley, with the four wolves following like obedient dogs.

Bagheera looked at Baloo. 'What do you think of our little cub now?'

'He is almost grown up,' said Baloo.

Moving as silently as shadows, Mowgli led his wolf brothers towards Buldeo, but they kept hidden. Then they saw that Buldeo had come to the place where Akela had messed up their tracks.

'What's this?' he muttered. 'Have wolves been dancing here?' Buldeo didn't know which way to go. Then a group of charcoal burners* came along the track.

'Are you out hunting?' they asked Buldeo.

'I am indeed hunting,' said Buldeo. 'I am hunting a jungle boy whose mother is a witch* and whose father is a wizard.'

'What?!' whispered Mowgli, but the wolves hushed him.

'Tell us what he is saying!' whispered the wolves, because of course they couldn't understand the language of men.

Buldeo told the charcoal burners how Mowgli had come out of the jungle. 'The boy had turned himself into a wolf! And he bewitched my gun so that the bullet bent in its flight and hit and killed my best buffalo! We have the boy's parents shut into their hut and we will kill them.'

'When?' asked the charcoal burners.

'When I have caught and killed the wolf-boy we will burn the witch and wizard. Then I will have all their buffaloes, which are particularly fine ones. And I will tell the authorities that the woman and man died of snake bites.'

'Well,' said the charcoal burners. 'The sun is going down and we don't want to spend the night in this jungle. We'll go to your village and see for ourselves what a witch looks like!'

'I'll come with you,' said Buldeo. 'You need someone with a gun to protect you while that wild wolf-boy is about!'

Mowgli heard all this. He told his wolf brothers, 'My man mother and father are trapped by the men in the village. The people plan to kill them because of me. So I must go and free them. Will you delay Buldeo and the other men for me, brothers? Then come and meet me in the village.'

Grey Brother grinned. 'We will enjoy it!' he said. 'We will sing to them and twist them around in circles of fear! My panther brother will help me.'

Bagheera had arrived silently. Now he lifted his head and growl-howled into the jungle.

'What was that?' asked the men, clutching one another.

'Thank you, my brothers!' laughed Mowgli, and he ran towards the village.

Mowgli could hear the wolves and Bagheera howling to sound like a whole pack of wolves as he hurried down into the village. He sneaked through the gateway, and went to Messua's hut and found it guarded by two men. But Mowgli prowled to the back of the hut and slipped through the window.

Inside, he found Messua and her husband bound and gagged and hurt. Quickly and quietly, Mowgli sliced through the ropes. He clasped a hand over Messua's mouth to stop her from calling out, then he let her speak.

'My son!' she said. 'You have come to save us! What a good boy you are!'

'You must go now!' said Mowgli. 'Run away to another village! They are going to come and kill you!'

Messua's husband was afraid. 'But how can we survive out in the jungle?' he said. 'The animals will hunt us, and so will the people. There is no way to escape!'

Just then they heard shouting and running feet.

'Buldeo is back,' said Mowgli. 'I will go and see what is happening.'

Out through the window went Mowgli, then he hid in the shadow of the huts and saw the people gathered under the peepul tree.

Buldeo was telling his tale. 'There is wicked magic in the jungle!' he told the crowd. 'It is the fault of the wolf-boy and his parents! They must be punished! They must be burned!'

Something damp touched Mowgli's foot. 'Mother Wolf!'

Mother Wolf told Mowgli, 'I will help if I can. I care about the woman who cared for you, my son.' She looked Mowgli firmly in the eye. 'But remember, my Mowgli. I gave you more milk than she ever did!'

Mowgli smiled and touched Mother Wolf's head. 'I know that,' he said.

Mowgli helped the two frightened people out through the window of their hut. He told them, 'Now run!'

We will go to the town thirty miles away,' said Messua, 'if only we can get safely through the jungle tonight.'

'I promise you will be safe,' said Mowgli. He told Mother Wolf, 'Send a message to our jungle friends to say that these people must not be hurt.'

Mother Wolf's long howl cut through the
night. Messua's husband wanted to climb back
into the hut. But his wife stopped him. She
told him, 'Trust our son.'

So the man and woman went into the
darkness, guarded and guided by wolves.

'Bagheera?' said Mowgli to the darkness.

'I am here, little brother,' said Bagheera, his
dark shape detaching from the shadows. 'Shall
I kill the other people now?' Bagheera's eyes
glittered with thoughts of hunting.

'No,' said Mowgli. 'We might tease them,
but we will not kill them.'

The people of the village were noisy under the peepul tree. They were yelling and preparing to come with their sticks and clubs and knives to find Messua and her husband.

'Kill the witch and the wizard!' they shouted.

Bagheera grinned wide. 'Put me in the trap where they expect to find your man parents!'

Mowgli laughed. 'I will!'

So Bagheera was settled on the bed in the hut as the people battered down the door. Bagheera was so long he dripped over the ends of the bed, but he lay there with front paws crossed and a smile on his black face. In burst the people, shouting and waving weapons.

They saw Bagheera.

They stopped still.

They screamed and they ran, tripping over one another, pushing and struggling to escape the big black panther.

Bagheera slowly rose up and yawned wide, his mouth full of magnificent white teeth and curled red tongue. And by the time he poured

himself back out through the window, the street was empty. 'They will not come out of their huts again tonight,' he told Mowgli. 'I will stay and make sure of it. You need to sleep, man-cub.'

So Mowgli slept on a rock in the jungle while the wolves and the panther kept watch over jungle and village. He was woken next morning by Bagheera with a fresh-killed deer for breakfast, and some news. 'Chil says that your man parents have arrived at the town, and are safe.'

'That is good,' smiled Mowgli.

'So, come, little brother,' said Bagheera. 'Baloo has some hives and he wants to harvest the honey. Let us forget all about people and enjoy our jungle again!'

CHAPTER 9

— ◆ —

Mowgli has to choose

When spring arrived the year that Mowgli was seventeen, something changed in him. He felt restless and sad and weary in a way he never had before. Akela was dead, and so were Mowgli's wolf parents. He still had his wolf brothers, and Baloo and Bagheera and Kaa, but it felt to Mowgli as if something was missing. He was cross and he didn't know why.

'I must get away from this place for a while,' thought Mowgli. 'I'll go to the marshland and spend some time there.'

So Mowgli ran and swung and leaped and

twisted his way through the jungle, and out of the jungle, across the plain, to the marshland where nobody knew him. He jumped the grassy tussocks* across the black, watery marsh, and he settled amongst the long reeds.

He'd enjoyed feeling his strength as he ran, but now, alone in the reeds, Mowgli found that his sadness had come with him. How can I ever get happy again? he wondered. Then he remembered what wise old Akela had told him. 'One day you will go back and live as a man.' Was that true? wondered Mowgli.

His thinking led to him wandering one night, across the plain to another man-village. The flames of Red Flower flared beside one hut. Mowgli went close, and the dogs chained to the hut barked into the night.

'Grrr!' Mowgli wolf-growled to silence them.

But the sound woke a woman, who came to the hut door. She spoke to a child inside the hut. 'It was only a jackal, and it has gone now.'

Mowgli began to shake all over when he heard that voice. 'Messua!' he said.

'Who is it?' asked the woman.

'Have you forgotten your son?' asked Mowgli.

The woman put a hand to her heart. 'If you are truly my son, then tell me the name that I gave you.'

'Nathoo!' said Mowgli, and he came out of the night to stand in the firelight.

Messua's hair was grey, but her voice was the same. Mowgli was tall and his hair was long over his shoulders, but his mother knew him. 'Your father is dead, but you have a brother now. Come inside and meet him.'

Messua led Mowgli into the hut, where a small child looked at Mowgli with big eyes. Messua brought cups of milk for each of her boys, and then she put them to bed.

Mowgli slept long into the next day. When he woke, Messua wanted to comb his hair and talk to him and find out where he had been and what he had been doing. But Mowgli heard a noise from outside the hut. It was Grey Brother.

'I'm coming!' said Mowgli, and he got up to go.

'Oh, don't leave us!' pleaded Messua. 'Stay with us!'

Mowgli hesitated, but his wolf brother called again, and he did go, back to his jungle home.

Grey Brother asked crossly, 'Why have you returned to a man pack?'

'I don't know why,' said Mowgli.

So the wolf family and Kaa and old Baloo

met at Council Rock to discuss what Mowgli
should do now.

Mowgli looked at them all. 'I love you, but
I feel a pull towards the village too. My man
father is dead. I have a small brother there
who needs someone to teach him how to live.'

Baloo put a paw on Mowgli's shoulder. 'Then you can teach him all that I have taught you, Little Frog. It is time you made your own track and your own lair. It is time for you to teach your own cubs.'

'You are shedding an old skin,'* said Kaa. 'That is all.'

'But Mowgli belongs in our pack!' said Grey Brother. 'Remember how Bagheera gave a dead bull to pay for Mowgli to join the pack?'

There was a sudden roar and a crash, and there was Bagheera, his mouth and paws red with fresh blood.

'And here is another bull, fresh-killed,' he said. 'This bull pays for Mowgli's release.' Bagheera bent and licked Mowgli's foot. 'Remember that Bagheera loved you, man-cub!' And he bounded away into the forest.

Baloo reached for Mowgli and bear-hugged him.

'Come here, my lovely boy!'

Mowgli clung to Baloo and sobbed.

But as dawn was opening the jungle to a new day, Mowgli was making his way back to the village, where a little man-cub needed to be cared for.

Rudyard Kipling
(born 1865, died 1936)

Rudyard Kipling was a popular author and poet. He was born in India and when he was six he was sent to England to go to school. He had to live with people he did not know and was very unhappy. Perhaps this move to a very different way of life inspired his idea of a boy escaping into the jungle.

When he was 16, he moved back to India where he worked as a journalist. He spoke some Hindustani which is a mix of Urdu and Hindi. In his spare time, he began to write books. In 1892 he married an American woman and moved to the United States of America.

Kipling started writing *The Jungle Book* and other children's stories just after his first child, Josephine, was born. Tragically, Josephine died of 'flu when she was just six-years-old, and his only son died at 18, in the First World War. Kipling spent the later part of his life as a famous celebrity in England, but never recovered from the loss of his children. He was survived by his wife and younger daughter, Elsie.

He was awarded the nobel prize in Literature in 1907.

Best known works

Books	Poems
The Jungle Book	*If*
Just So Stories	*Gunga Din*
Kim	*Mandalay*

Pippa Goodhart

Pippa grew up in Granchester, Cambridgeshire – a village where the school playground was partly meadow shared with cows. She had cats, a dog and a pond with newts and fish in it, so she has always lived with animals, even if they weren't jungle ones!

When she left school she studied History at Leeds University, then worked in Heffers Children's Bookshop in Cambridge for five years. She finally began to write books when she became a mum at home with small children. Her first book was published in 1994. She has written over fifty books, ranging from picture books to novels. All have been her own stories. Her best known book is *You Choose* (see her website: www.pippagoodhart.co.uk).

The Jungle Book is the first time she has rewritten somebody else's story. She says, 'I wasn't sure I was going to enjoy doing that, but it was fun. I left out bits from the original story that I thought were boring or too cruel or strange, and I concentrated on the story of Mowgli as somebody who wasn't completely animal or completely human in his upbringing – he was just himself.'

Notes about this book

At the time the book was written much of India was covered in jungle. People cleared areas of the jungle to make villages and fields. They surrounded their villages with thorn fences to keep out wild animals from the jungle. Kipling had never visited the area of India in which the book is set. He researched the jungle by reading books about it.

When Kipling was in India there were several news stories about children who had been brought up by wolves. These reports may have been the idea for *The Jungle Book*.

The book has been used as the basis for several films and TV series. The most famous is Walt Disney's 1967 cartoon, *The Jungle Book*. The film changes the book quite a lot. For example, in the film Kaa is a 'baddie', whereas in the book the python is Mowgli's friend and teacher.

Page 5
* **Shere Khan** 'Tiger Lord'. 'Sher' means lion or tiger, and 'Khan' means lord.

Page 9
* **Mowgli** A word made up by Kipling, which means 'frog'.

Page 10
* **Akela** Means 'alone' in Hindi and Urdu. The leader of a troop of Boy Scouts is called 'Akela', after this leader of the wolf pack in *The Jungle Book*.
* **Baloo** 'Bear'. 'Bhaloo' means bear in Hindi and Urdu.

***Bagheera** 'Baagh' means tiger in Hindi and Urdu, and Kipling used this word to create the name Bagheera for the panther in the story.

Page 16
***Chil** In Hindi and Urdu 'chiil' means bird of prey. In this story Chil is a type of bird of prey called a kite.

Page 17
***Kaa** A name made up by Kipling. He took it from the hissing noise made by large snakes.

Page 18
***Lost City** Refers to one of many deserted cities in the Indian jungle.

Page 33
***Hammock** Chimpanzees make 'nests' like this in trees every night.

Page 39
***Hackles** The hairs on the back of a wolf's neck that stand up when they are angry.

Page 45
***Village elder** An older person who is highly respected in the village.
***Peepul tree** A big fig tree with a massive trunk that provides shade. These trees could be used as a meeting place in a village.
***Ghost tiger** Shere Khan the tiger had a limp. Buldeo, who is very superstitious, believes that Shere Khan is the ghost of an old man from the village who also had a limp.

Page 48
* **Avalanche** When snow, ice and rocks suddenly fall down a mountainside.

Page 50
* **Maharaja** The title given to an Indian king.

Page 57
* **Charcoal burners** People who move from forest to forest making charcoal by burning wood and selling it to local people.

Page 58
* **Witch** Buldeo believes that things he doesn't understand are magic. He calls Messua a witch because he believes she is the mother of a child with magic powers – Mowgli.

Page 70
* **Grassy tussocks** Thick tufts of grass.

Page 74
* **Shedding an old skin** When a snake slithers out of its outer layer of skin from time to time. This takes off the old skin and allows the snake to grow.